SYMBOLS OF THE UNITED STATES

Uncle Sam

Helen Lepp Friesen
and Heather Kissock

AV2

www.openlightbox.com

AV2

Step 1
Go to **www.openlightbox.com**

Step 2
Enter this unique code
AMCGINKE6

Step 3
Explore your interactive eBook!

AV2 is optimized for use on any device

Your interactive eBook comes with...

Audio Listen to the entire book read aloud

Videos Watch informative video clips

Weblinks Gain additional information for research

Try This! Complete activities and hands-on experiments

Key Words Study vocabulary, and complete a matching word activity

Quizzes Test your knowledge

Slideshows View images and captions

Share Share titles within your Learning Management System (LMS) or Library Circulation System

Citation Create bibliographical references following APA, CMOS, and MLA styles

This title is part of our AV2 digital subscription

1-Year Texas Subscription
ISBN 978-1-5105-8659-8

Access hundreds of AV2 titles with our digital subscription.
Sign up for a FREE trial at **www.openlightbox.com/trial**

The digital components of this book are guaranteed to stay active for at least five years from the date of publication.

Uncle Sam

CONTENTS

A NATIONAL SYMBOL

Uncle Sam is a symbol of the United States.

He stands for the country and its people.

WEARING THE FLAG

Uncle Sam has long white hair and a beard.

His clothes are red, white, and blue. These are the colors of the American flag.

SAMUEL WILSON
1766 · 1854
TROY
MENOTOMY
8

THE REAL UNCLE SAM

The symbol of Uncle Sam came from a real man.

His name was Samuel Wilson.

Samuel Wilson lived in **Troy, New York**. This town is now known as the "**Home of Uncle Sam**."

FOOD FOR SOLDIERS

Samuel Wilson sent meat to soldiers during the War of 1812.

The meat was placed in barrels marked "U.S." This stood for "United States."

A NEW NICKNAME

The soldiers started to say that "U.S." stood for "Uncle Sam."

Uncle Sam soon became a nickname for the United States.

Uncle Sam is also the **name** of the **largest diamond ever found** in the **United States**.

A SYMBOL GROWS

Newspapers printed stories about Uncle Sam. Many artists made pictures of him.

The first pictures looked like Samuel Wilson.

CHANGING LOOKS

Pictures of Uncle Sam changed over time. He was shown as an older man.

He grew a beard. His clothing had stars and stripes.

During the **American Civil War**, **Uncle Sam** was drawn to **look like President Abraham Lincoln**.

"I WANT YOU"

One artist drew
Uncle Sam for a poster.

It was used to get people
to join the army.

JAMES MONTGOMERY FLAGG
I WANT YOU
FOR U.S. ARMY
NEAREST RECRUITING STATION

PENFIELD
1810
2010
BICENTENNIAL

UNCLE SAM TODAY

Today, Uncle Sam can be seen in newspaper cartoons, on posters, and in parades.

He is often seen at Fourth of July events.

September 13, 1989, was named **Uncle Sam Day** in honor of **Samuel Wilson's birthday**.

UNCLE SAM FACTS

These pages provide detailed information that expands on the interesting facts found in the book. They are intended to be used by adults as a learning support to help young readers round out their knowledge of each icon in the *Symbols of the United States* series.

Pages 4–5

A National Symbol

Uncle Sam is a symbol of the United States. A symbol is an image or picture that stands for something else. Uncle Sam is often used to represent the U.S. government. Cartoons and posters usually show Uncle Sam as a tall, slim, elderly man with stern eyes and white hair.

Pages 6–7

Wearing the Flag

Uncle Sam wears clothes that represent the American flag. Most commonly, he wears a red and white striped top hat with white stars on blue trim. His goatee beard is pointy and white. He wears a white shirt with a red bow tie under a blue coat. Red and white striped pants finish the outfit.

Pages 8–9

The Real Uncle Sam

The real Uncle Sam was a man named Samuel Wilson. He was born in Massachusetts, in 1766. Raised on a farm for most of his life, Wilson decided on a different career track for himself. Along with his brother Ebenezer, he moved to Troy, New York. There, Samuel and Ebenezer opened a meat-packing company called E. & S. Wilson.

Pages 10–11

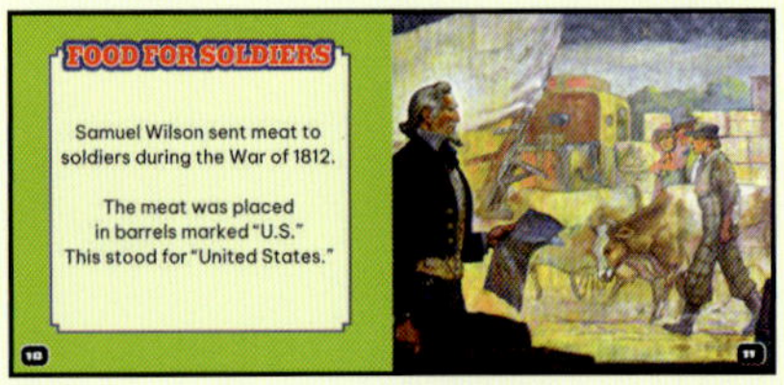

Food for Soldiers

During the War of 1812, a conflict between the United States and Great Britain, Samuel Wilson was eager to help his country. He and his brother earned a contract to provide meat for U.S. Army soldiers. The brothers packed the meat in barrels and marked each with the letters "U.S." This showed that the barrels were for the United States government.

Pages 12–13

A New Nickname

The people of Troy often referred to Wilson as Uncle Sam. When soldiers saw "U.S." marked on the barrels, they said the meat shipments came from Uncle Sam. A local newspaper ran a story about this. Soon, Uncle Sam became a nickname for the U.S. government.

Pages 14–15

A Symbol Grows

By 1813, Uncle Sam had become known across the country. On May 12, 1830, the New York Gazette printed a story connecting Samuel Wilson to the Uncle Sam character. Over time, many artists drew pictures of Uncle Sam. Some people thought the original cartoon of Uncle Sam looked like Samuel Wilson.

Pages 16–17

Changing Looks

The portrayal of Uncle Sam evolved over time. In the 1860s, during the American Civil War, he was often drawn to look like President Abraham Lincoln. A political cartoonist named Thomas Nast popularized the image of Uncle Sam with a white beard. Later cartoons did not resemble either Wilson or Lincoln.

Pages 18–19

"I Want You"

In 1916, James Montgomery Flagg drew the best-known poster of Uncle Sam. In the poster, Uncle Sam points his finger and says, "I want you for U.S. Army." More than four million posters were printed during World War I. They were used to recruit soldiers for the army. Flagg used his own face as the basis for his drawing of Uncle Sam.

Pages 20–21

Uncle Sam Today

In 1961, the United States Congress officially recognized Samuel Wilson as the man behind the American icon, Uncle Sam. The image of Uncle Sam has remained mostly unchanged since the 1960s. Today, Uncle Sam Day is celebrated on September 13 every year.

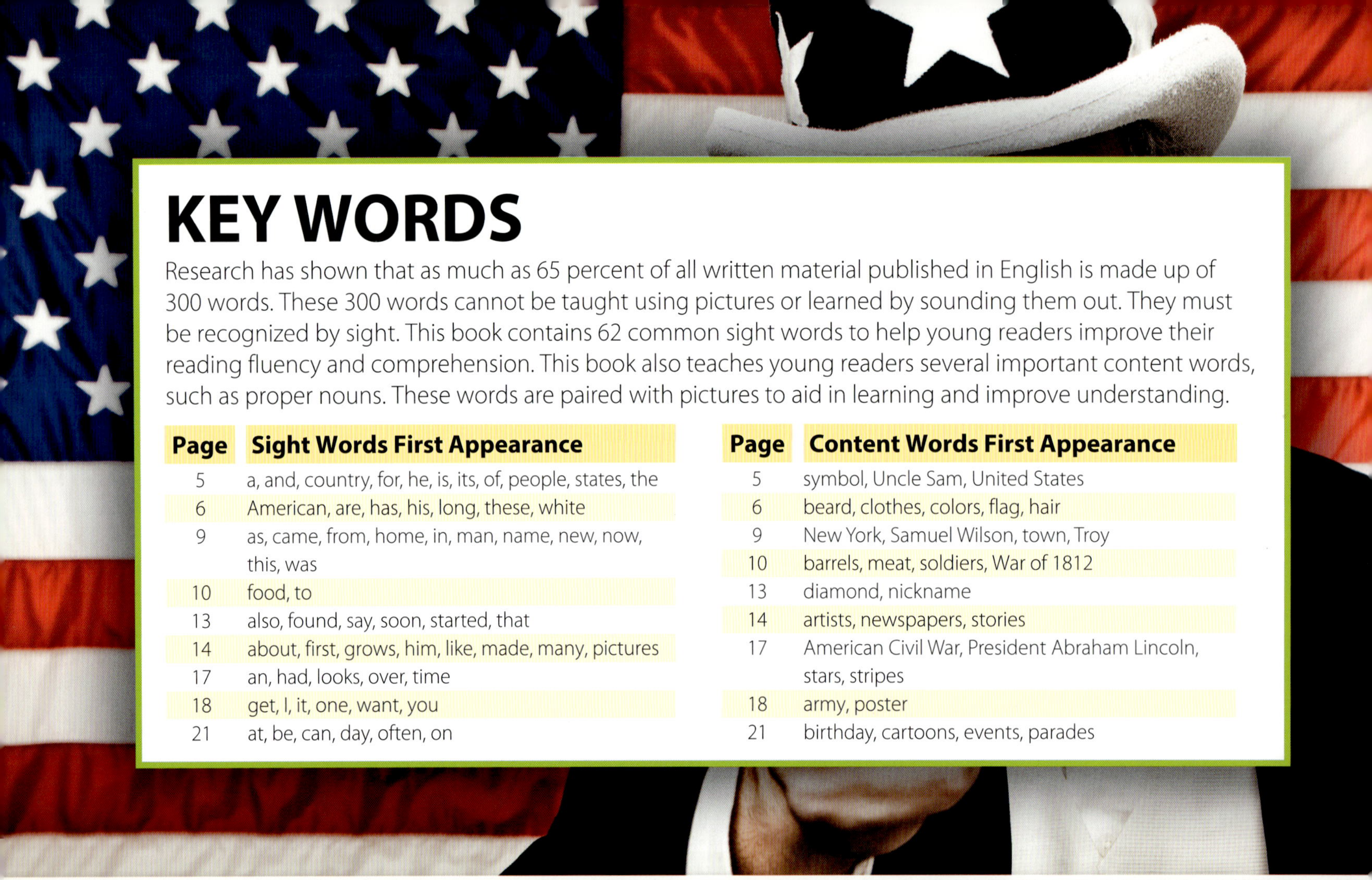

KEY WORDS

Research has shown that as much as 65 percent of all written material published in English is made up of 300 words. These 300 words cannot be taught using pictures or learned by sounding them out. They must be recognized by sight. This book contains 62 common sight words to help young readers improve their reading fluency and comprehension. This book also teaches young readers several important content words, such as proper nouns. These words are paired with pictures to aid in learning and improve understanding.

Page	Sight Words First Appearance
5	a, and, country, for, he, is, its, of, people, states, the
6	American, are, has, his, long, these, white
9	as, came, from, home, in, man, name, new, now, this, was
10	food, to
13	also, found, say, soon, started, that
14	about, first, grows, him, like, made, many, pictures
17	an, had, looks, over, time
18	get, I, it, one, want, you
21	at, be, can, day, often, on

Page	Content Words First Appearance
5	symbol, Uncle Sam, United States
6	beard, clothes, colors, flag, hair
9	New York, Samuel Wilson, town, Troy
10	barrels, meat, soldiers, War of 1812
13	diamond, nickname
14	artists, newspapers, stories
17	American Civil War, President Abraham Lincoln, stars, stripes
18	army, poster
21	birthday, cartoons, events, parades

Published by Lightbox Learning Inc.
276 5th Avenue, Suite 704 #917
New York, NY 10001
Website: www.openlightbox.com

Library of Congress Control Number: 2024938985

ISBN 978-1-5105-8327-6 (hardcover)
ISBN 979-8-8745-1500-3 (softcover)
ISBN 978-1-5105-8330-6 (static multi-user eBook)
ISBN 978-1-5105-8329-0 (interactive multi-user eBook)

Printed in Guangzhou, China
1 2 3 4 5 6 7 8 9 0 28 27 26 25 24

072024
100923

Project Coordinator: Priyanka Das
Designer: Terry Paulhus
Layout: Jean Faye Rodriguez

Every reasonable effort has been made to trace ownership and to obtain permission to reprint copyright material. The publisher would be pleased to have any errors or omissions brought to its attention so that they may be corrected in subsequent printings.

The publisher acknowledges Alamy, Getty Images, and Shutterstock as the primary image suppliers for this title.